Get Back Up Again

How to Cope When Down With Grief

By

Anchal Prasher

ISBN: 978-1-3999-4719-0

Cover design and images by: Anchal Prasher

London, UK

This book is dedicated to Joel S. Arnold

and our three children.

His Spirit lives on.

Contents

Introduction

It's said that there is a book in everyone. This is mine, the last six weeks of my life where my husband died and left me with three children aged 13, 10 & 6. It's a form of therapy for me, a way to unblock my throat chakra, to digest what has happened and how I've managed to keep focusing on the bright future ahead of me.

I've actively been working on increasing my vibration by sending out positive energy for the past twelve months. But also taking action on my self-care and self-love for the last three months. These two steps I've taken have allowed me to process, accept and understand the situation I'm faced with.

This is my journey and I welcome you to listen, take part and connect with me afterwards. I hope you take some ideas away and 'Get Back Up Again' when you're feeling down. Find me on all social media channels: (Anchal Prasher).

"When a person really desires something, all the universe conspires to help that person realise their dream"
- Paulo Coelho

PART I: WHAT HAPPENED

From 8th Dec 2022 to 2nd Feb 2023

CHAPTER 1:

8th Dec 2023

I'll just jump straight into the day that changed our futures, 8th of December 2023. We woke up and got dressed for school as usual that Thursday morning, unusually there was a beautiful, enormous, pink full moon in the sky. I took some photos and went around the house telling everyone they should admire it. We said goodbye to Joel and set off for school.

Joel had ligament damage to his ankle six months before, it was causing him a lot of discomfort and restricting his ability to walk or drive. So that morning he went back to bed as he had done for the previous few months.

I dropped off the kids and went to Aldi, a new one which I loved going to, so was happily getting our favourite foods without succumbing to the Christmas selections. I wanted to wait until the school holidays to break out all the treats.

I returned home two hours later unpacked the frozen food and went to ask Joel if he'd like a hot drink. I found that he wasn't with us anymore. He had died. I called an ambulance and they arrived within a few minutes but there was nothing that could be done. They'd done all their tests but sadly his heart had suddenly stopped. We still don't know the exact cause. Just a sudden cardiac arrest. He had died in his sleep. Joel looked calm and peaceful.

The whole day was spent with the paramedics and police officers. When a death occurs in the home the police must come and essentially fill in lots of forms. They set-up camp in the kitchen, there were about five paramedics and eight police officers. A lot of people in my small house. I felt so little in my new baggy purple joggers and oversized geometric jumper. I had asked if they would sit down but they said that their vest equipment stopped them from being able to do so. But they were all so nice, each one coming to ask more of their questions to find out what happened. I was glad to have the kittens to amuse them on this sad workday. There was only one thing I asked of them, would they all leave and take Joel away before the children were back from school. I did have options to take the kids elsewhere to tell them, but I wanted them to be at home and with the things that comfort them. I thought it was better that way.

During those initial hours I realised that I was in an incredibly sad situation. One where all my energy could be drained out leaving me with none, preventing me from looking after myself or the children and making the whole situation even worse. I was not strong; I was calm and focused on what needed to be done. Only what needed to be done about the children. Nothing else. I couldn't get sided tracked by the funeral, telling others, messages or phone calls. The next few days would just be about them. The rest could wait or someone else could help.

My brother-in-law had come a few hours after it had happened and my sister too. My constant thoughts were on how I could make it work. It was now very important to me that we were at home after school, I wondered how I was going to manage the logistics of multiple pick-ups and also the fact of telling them. The police worked hard for me and made my wishes come true. We managed to get the best outcome we could, I knew somehow it would work out. The time between picking up the eldest then waiting outside the younger ones school and realising that I had an opportunity to tell the school that they wouldn't be attending the Christmas carols concert and why. The drive home was strange, I was gearing up to be honest, clear and helpful. We would sit on the sofa and together we'd tell them.

The children were upset but seemed to understand the gravity of what we were telling them. I let them continue their evening as they chose, the usual, playing video games and watching YouTube. I made dinner that evening, but got mine and Joel's favourite Thai takeaway for me and my brother-in-law. Joel would have loved that food! We talked about him and thought about where his spirit and energy may have gone now that it had left his body.

That night my eldest slept on the floor mattress in the loft with my daughter and I, we have a huge loft light which my son slept under. He said, "I think dad's energy has gone into the moon as I've never seen it shining so brightly before". He was right, that full moon we saw that morning was now even bigger, so bright, illuminating the whole room. It was beautiful. Also, in the loft is a huge tiger plush which the children sit on. We decided that his spirit must have gone into a tiger, as it was his favourite animal, so again we had him there, looking out for us. We were calm that night knowing that Joel's energy was around us.

The children slept and so did I. I knew that I would need my sleep to be able to function well for them. To be calm and able to make decisions as I was sure there were lots of changes to the Christmas I was expecting.

Joel S. Arnold

1979-2022

His spirit lives on

CHAPTER 2:

The Next Day to Eight Weeks On

My middle child said to me the night Joel died "Mum I need to go to school tomorrow, I can't let the hockey team down, I have a maths paper to do, and I have my Primary maths challenge results to receive". I said of course you must go if that's what you feel. I couldn't believe what I was hearing, I was so proud that he was strong and resilient to even think about it. The next day went well, he actually ended up getting man of the match and Silver in his Maths challenge. I was so proud, and Joel would have been too.

That conversation made me address my own needs for the next day. Was I going to be strong and resilient like him? I felt I would keep my needs and wants clear, have a positive mindset and a growth mindset. Just as they teach at school. He set up my mind to keep moving forward and do it with pride and positivity

Initially I was worried about how he would manage at school, but I hadn't needed to worry. I felt like I had left him with family. After informing the head of pastoral care the day it happened, she quickly arranged a leadership team meeting and said that it was likely he would come to school and that she would arrange cover for all her lessons so she could be available at any time. She even accompanied him to the hockey away match. I couldn't have been prouder of the school that they go to. All my fears alleviated; they were treating my son as if he was their own.

The weekend came by and cousins and friends visited which was fun for the kids and a relief for me. I kept all of them at home for the next seven days, middle child couldn't understand why he was allowed to be off school and was worrying about his 100% attendance. I had to explain that other people, adults were taking compassionate leave from work, and it was absolutely fine to take some time to process a big change that has happened. The last two days of the winter term are the best with Christmas dinner, Santa and a disco. They all went to school which for me was good for me, it was nice to have the usual routine back but also get over the hurdle of going back to school. I felt that leaving it until after the holidays might make it more challenging. They all had positive days, with friends and teachers being very supportive.

For me seeing parents at the school gates was a bit daunting. I knew everyone would want to speak to me, hug me and support me. But I was thinking negatively about it, I didn't want to be the centre of attention, I didn't want people to give me 'the look', when thinking about it I found it really difficult. But I decided that everyone would want to be kind to me, help me and I was going to actively take each and every hug and all the positive energy it came with, and accept the love and support being given to me and the children. It worked, I loved it, it cemented all the love and support I got through the messages with the power of touch, hugs and squeezes! Chatting to the people I see most days was so therapeutic and I didn't realise how much it would help. It was a lovely way to see off the winter term and get ready for Christmas. That last day off without the kids helped me to prepare myself mentally for the next three weeks of the Christmas holidays and all that it would bring.

My sister and brother-in-law and then my parents were with us during day for the weeks that followed. I didn't want to go anywhere else just stay with our things; our memories and it felt safe. My family and friends bought lots of food and we got far too much takeaway, but we were able to enjoy it together and the children and I could appreciate the effort everyone around us was making.

During these first two weeks I tried to keep our plans going so I didn't cancel my Chinese acupuncture session as it was a positive thing to do. I also returned books at the library with the kids. We finished off the Christmas shopping (I was so proud I had most of it done before December, I wanted to be one of 'those people'!) but needed more Christmas spirit than ever so I welcomed the change of thoughts. A week after Joel died the two younger ones went to school to enjoy the Christmas lunch and disco, while the eldest and I sought our first real Christmas tree! It was huge, exactly as tall as the ceiling, we got it and some new blue decorations all for half price, which was win! So, we had our Christmas ready. I'll also say I got a beautiful wreath that Joel would have loved. One with cinnamon and oranges, I wanted it to be magical for the children but also when family and friends came to visit, it would smell lovely.

The funeral was to be after Christmas (something I really wanted and somehow within this busy time I got our chosen date), so I felt we should enjoy ourselves, have a different Christmas. A sad 'blue' Christmas but surrounded by family who we normally wouldn't have spent it with. It was calm, relaxed and full of presents. There were magical fairy lights and kittens in the tree, we had a good time. Full of love and treats!

Before the funeral we thought long and hard about what we wanted to happen that day. Which ceremonies we would have? How would we manage the families and friends who wanted to pay their condolences? How much would it cost? What were the processes from the coroner to the funeral director then crematorium? The main thing I thought about was the children. How would the day go well for them? What would make it easiest for them? But also, what do I want to happen? How can I integrate that with what his brother and family want?

It played out well. I'd tried to be open to conversation and discussion on religious beliefs, ceremonies and ideas everyone had on the running of the day. I felt as though I got what I wanted and everyone else was happy too. We decided to have smaller gatherings, Joel's cousins hosted a memorial dinner for his side of the family. Joel's cousins, aunts and uncles were to view his coffin at the funeral parlour and pay their respects. The dinner was lovely, the children played while the adults chatted about all the old memories, the love and positivity given out by everyone that evening was so uplifting but of course it was very sad.

We decided that only the closest family from both sides would attend the cremation. And that I was the only one to speak. We had half an hour so thought I could manage that for the children. Well actually I didn't, I had contingency plans for each part I didn't complete or couldn't manage. But I had the ambition that I would manage it.

Joel wasn't religious and nor am I. He would have said he's spiritual, me too. So, I wanted to reflect on those ideas at the crematorium with songs that would uplift us and stories that would show him off with his love for adventure and kindness towards others. That was the plan but if I couldn't speak, I'd just play the music, if the music didn't work, we'd just sit in silence and be calm in the moment. I knew everything was going to be ok. In the end I'd only half written the speech, I couldn't write it all down, there were twenty-six years of memories. Instead, I had keywords to remind me, and I just talked about them from my heart. I really liked that we thanked his body for being the vessel that carried his soul and I said that this was the first part of the funeral, creating ashes from his body, the second is scattering them in the most beautiful place on earth to complete the circle of life. My song choices were Thousand Miles by Vanessa Carlton, Step by step by Whitney Houston,

Just Sing (Trolls World Tour) by Anna Kendrick and James Cordon and Heaven (Candlelight mix) By DJ Sammy.

It had to be for the children, I told them to look around the room and see their family, the ones who will support us any time we need. I told Joel that he should rest as we're well looked after and that we're ok.

I also did a few quirky things, while Step by Step was playing I handed around a few large smooth rocks we found in Scotland. I wanted us to firstly feel the weight of something heavy, the texture and beauty and as the song says, stone-by-stone, brick-by-brick we'll make it. I love my rock collection, it gives me joy. I also wanted to have the presence of the moon as we felt his energy was there. I printed my keywords on the back of a photograph I took (the one after the introduction page). My shoes were comfy and designed for the Mexican Day of the Dead festival, they were fuchsia and mustard coloured. And they had 'Para Mi Familia' written on them, it just made the day even more special as Joel was all for his family.

I was empowered afterwards, I felt that Joel would have been proud of me. How I overcame fears that I had about speaking in public at such an event. The praise I got from my family was also lovely to hear. I was grateful for how it went.

Although I'm not religious I do love singing Hare Krishna songs and absolutely love the temple in Watford, Hertfordshire. I had planned a visit there following the cremation. They have acres of land with a lake, peacocks and herons. There is a manicured garden and trail walk. A playground and a café for the children. I wanted to make it special for my children, to show them the support that our families were giving us. All their closest cousins came to the temple to sing and eat with us. We had a walk around the beautiful grounds, I asked them to sit in the temple and sing for ten minutes then go and play. I meanwhile let loose on the chanting of 'Hare Krishna Hare Krishna, Krishna Krishna Hare Hare', the devotees cheering everyone on to sing louder and louder, everyone clapping and dancing. The energy was amazing. I was so grateful to be in that environment in that beautiful space. It was so memorable.

The third and final part of the funeral was back at home. Initially, when we first discussed it, I didn't want anyone coming to my house. I didn't want the disruption, but I came to understand that it was a good thing. I imagined all the positive energy in house, the warmth of love and support right here where we live, where we lost Joel. It made sense, I'd felt so some much positive energy through their messages, wouldn't it be fantastic to have them here for real hugs. It made it fair for the children too, they could all play upstairs and have fun while we do the 'adulting'. I did it my way though. We had a playlist on, which was made collaboratively by lots of family and friends, a video photo carousel playing on a computer I had moved to the kitchen. I thought that everyone likes to hang out in the kitchen so it would be a great spot to remember Joel. I put up every piece of my art that I could, Joel would have loved to have seen that. He was always encouraging me to put them up. I found his hammer and nails and got to work.

Now Christmas was over I put the Christmas tree outside near the front door with the lights on, a table next to it with Joel's photo and hand decorated tea light holders which said 'thankful' and Joel's name on them. I wanted to show my appreciation to everyone that came and supported us. It was therapeutic making them, writing 'Thankful' many times is always a good thing!

I was pleased with how the day went. I think the children will look back and see it as a day to be remembered positively.

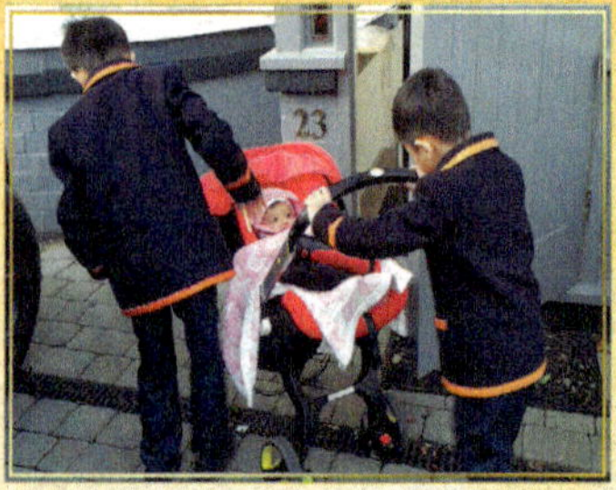
23

11

GAP

BW54
ARF

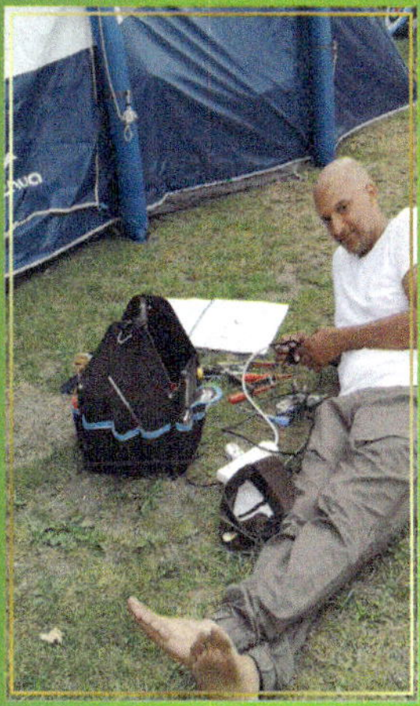

CHAPTER 3:

Control: What My Mind Did

I needed to maintain control. Control of the carriage I was riding with my three horses in front and now holding onto two reins (with the kittens and cat in the back). No one could get aboard unless preauthorised, the direction we were going to go in was down to me and only me. That was the big picture, but in real life that meant knowing what I want, what Joel would have wanted and what the kids want. Nothing else, no one else. I listened to advice and comments and then decided.

I realised that I would have to decide lots of things in the next, well forever, but you know funeral arrangements to begin with. I decided that I would need new comfy clothes and fluffy pyjamas. I was going to stay at home a lot and needed to feel safe and cosy. Especially since the snow had fallen! Now I was comfy, I needed to be calm. Calm at all times, 'if you're calm then you can think and then decide rather than just react'. If I ever felt that I was starting to get annoyed or disappointed about something I would take a breath and think about it, really digest every point of view then take action and move on from it in a calm manner.

When it came to visitors, I learnt that the people I wanted to come to my home were only the ones my children knew. It wasn't fair if they didn't feel able to move freely in the house, not wanting to say hello. I changed things so it was only me they were seeing; the children could be out somewhere having fun with friends or cousins. I controlled who interacted with my children. It needed to be people who they could enjoy the company of and give a positive outlook on the situation we were now in. I also didn't want my days to be taken up with visitors, the children and I needed to be in each other's company most of all.

Food was something that I needed to control. I had spent the previous three months working on maintaining a good household. Ensuring food was bought and used, not wasted. That mostly healthy meals were eaten, and we had family time in the evening everyday playing games and chatting. So, when Joel died everything changed. As I told you I had just been doing the weekly shop so had a fridge full of food. We then got takeaways and had gifts of bags of food. Of course, I was grateful, but it was difficult to see the waste and kitchen space being taken over. Luckily, I managed not to comfort eat especially as it was Christmas. I maintained that control and started managing the kitchen after the funeral. Getting my kitchen back was so important to me. Six weeks later I still have two boxes of long-life food. I'm a very lucky lady to be given so much.

When I was asked to make a photo reel of Joel for the memorial dinner with his extended family I said "No, I don't want to" I felt like I didn't want anyone to comment on him. After thinking about it I thought to ask for photos of him with them. I wanted to make it less about me and Joel but them and Joel. I also didn't want to look through my photos and go through the memories. I kept calm and thought more about my initial reaction which I think was unfair but decided that I could choose the photos that would illicit great comments and make Joel shine with my choices. So, I did that and kept my control. I thought it through and although it took a few days to get to the right decision I was pleased with the process and outcome.

It took eight hours to look through all my photos on Google, I didn't get to Dropbox; the really old photos. But I managed to get nearly 1000 photos of him doing something fun and exciting! He was full of adventure always learning and pushing himself to be better. The photo I chose to print for the funeral was one of him standing on top of our Land Rover on the border of France and Spain with the atmospheric clouds above the Pyrenees Mountains behind and in his outstretched arm he's holding a machete. I mean isn't that the ultimate photo!

That eight hours was tough, trawling through fifteen years of memories and I take a lot of photos! We went on so many epic adventures around Europe. I saw the good memories but also remembered the difficult ones. It was very therapeutic, and time well spent consolidating faded memories with the newly found photos. I felt so much gratitude to have had those experiences and the photos to remind the children (and everyone else) about his life.

On the day of the funeral, I was proud to have that photo carousel showing on the monitor, I now wanted to share and talk about the memories as they scrolled past. Although I was negative with my first thoughts about the photos, I remained calm and didn't get annoyed with the question. I said, "Let me think about it and get back to you". I gave myself time to really think it through. What was the problem and why am I against it? And then I did it in my own time and I was so happy that it was exactly how I wanted it. I was glad to include our family and friends by asking them for their photos and laughing at the memories they brought up. I was glad that I had the strength to spend hours daily finding the photos, it made me feel closer to him, remembering conversations and dilemmas we faced in those snapshot moments.

CHAPTER 4:

Triggers

From the moment it happened I knew that everything around me would trigger me and remind me of what I had lost. It was clear that I had to address this issue before it became overwhelming. But before that, I needed to leave everything in its place, the mess, the clutter and usual chaos in the house. It needed to stay the same. One change was big enough. Some family members were thinking the opposite to clean and clear the clutter, rearrange shelves, under the sofa and move his clothes. I wasn't happy with these suggestions but thought that I must allow others to process in the way that felt right for them. But for me I wanted his usual presence in the house and minimal disruption for me and the children.

Over the next week and before Christmas I did declutter the house but, in my time, and the way I wanted. I needed to maintain control of the situation. I also wanted it tidy and clean for the funeral. The way Joel would have wanted it if he had known the number of people who would be in the house. I was sure I could manage it and then I would also feel comfortable inviting many friends and family who had never been to my home. It felt like a big responsibility to represent Joel and what he had achieved with his home and family. I put up my artwork, moved furniture but really in my mind I was getting ready for the New Year as well as all my new visitors who I was delighted to welcome.

From not wanting to move anything to moving everything was a big jump. I felt empowered by my strength to make it happen. But I found it was an easy one as everyone (my children) could see and benefit from the work I was doing.

I'd finally mastered running the house with three kids and three cats. I wasn't going to let Joel's death to stop my work. I knew that if I did, life would become even harder.

I knew there was a potential for everything around me to trigger me, to remember something about Joel and our time with him. We've lived in our house for fifteen years; we've changed the house so much from the actual bricks and mortar to multiple pets and quite a few children. The memories are everywhere in my neighbourhood, the whole of London and lots of Europe. I was going to be triggered I knew that, but how was I going to manage it and make it a positive experience? After all it was going to happen multiple times a day. I started with what I thought was the hardest one, songs, Christmas songs. All of a sudden 'All I want for Christmas' by Mariah Carey just sounded so much sadder especially 'One More Sleep' by Leona Lewis, gosh they got me started. But I had to sing, I knew I had to open my throat chakra and let my voice be heard. The day after he died, I sang, I started making a playlist with the Grenfell Tower version of 'Bridge Over Troubled Water', wow that song hits a hard too, Fire and Water by Stormzy really helped me, his soulful voice and deep meaningful words were so comforting. I let the sad songs remind me of him and remind me that so many have suffered loss and sadness and I'm not alone. I needed to desensitise myself from the raw emotions the songs brought up. If I allowed them to take over my emotions, how would I ever listen to music again; it would be too hard. Seven weeks on and I'm able to listen, enjoy and sing the whole playlist which now is nearly nine hours of long. I wanted to include my family and friends in my journey with music. I shared a link so they could collaborate on the playlist, everyone wanted to help me and it was nice to give them something to do, something that was important to me. I've also made a playlist in my name, this one only has uplifting songs, and ones that give me energy and remind me how far I've come. I make time for sad songs but need the motivating ones more.

Long lost friends or blast-from-the-past messages were creating thoughts and activating memories that had long been forgotten. They came with two sides, a good and a bad. I felt like my brain was working in overdrive thinking so much about what 'has been'. Although I enjoyed looking back and remembering events and holidays and reconnecting with people who I thought I would never speak to again. It amazed me that people wanted to message me. Reconnecting 'under the circumstances' was a strange and sad place to be but I was grateful that, although we did not chat or meet up, their energy towards me was so strong. It was an amazing twist from the Universe. The grapevine is a strong, far reaching messaging service, I felt like I 'went viral'.

I realised I had been stopping myself from looking at the Dropbox folders, apart from the 'forgot password' situation, I didn't want to look at photos from when we first met 26 years ago to 2012. That was going to be tough. This week, week eight I made time and enjoyed all the emotions they brought up. The video phones back in the olden days were such bad quality. But so nice to see us foot-loose and fancy-free enjoying our life together. We had a lot of fun back then and while the kids were little. Life got in the way after that, but I still have thousands of memories I can call upon at any time through something I see in the street or memories that pop into my brain. I'm so grateful to have them. Now photos are good for me they allow me to disappear in a thought and enjoy the moment to feel connected.

My children are huge triggers, the way they look, speak and the things they do remind me of him. Also, when I'm looking after them, I know what Joel did with them, things that I sometimes have difficulty with. The children are kind to me, but I know how sad it is for them. I look at the youngest and her new front teeth are coming out and know that Joel will never see them. That the boys are looking more grown up now and he'll never know how proud he would be of them. But then I remember that I believe he will see them and be around us through good times and more bad times. He'll be guiding me in how to help them. To be honest his spirit has come to me when I should be drying their hair more or ironing the uniform properly. He keeps me calm in the morning school rush; I sense his energy. Maybe it's the fact that we were always in each other's pockets, we were basically living in lockdown together for twelve years. We spent nearly all our time together working or looking after the kids. We spent a lifetime together; if you compared it to how much time normal couples spend together. I will have my wonderful children for the rest of my lifetime reminding me of my wonderful husband.

When I was sending my messages back to everyone I would refer to or mention one of these triggers, I would use positive language and talk about how I'm moving forward. I needed to reinforce the positive effect of the triggers. At week eight I'm able to manage any thoughts and feeling that come up, able to understand them, acknowledge or accept them and if required take a positive action. If negative feelings remain then I 'phone a friend' discuss it and take an action. Those negative thoughts take up a lot of time and energy and should be resolved as soon as possible. There were many things that happened which I spent time wondering a lot about. I decided that I would take action, message the person first and say what I was feeling. It felt much better afterwards but also when I got a reply to resolve the issue, I felt a weight had been lifted and I could think clearly again. No matter the size of negative energy, it needs to go.

There's one thing that only triggers me positively and that's seeing the moon and the energy it brings. Knowing that the moon is there every day even if it's hiding, it is like knowing that Joel's energy and spirit is there. He's around us, not always visible but sometimes shining so brightly through the windows that we can't sleep. It's strange to believe this but I wholeheartedly do, he can't have just disappeared, his energy did go somewhere, and I believe his went to the moon. One day, maybe with Elon we'll go and visit him.

Food was a constant in my journey, there was always feeding to be done; three meals plus snacks but there was more to it, I've found that there were so many triggers with food, and I've been thinking about my attachments to them. From the initial visit to Aldi the morning it happened and then the next visit to get the snacks and drinks for the funeral to the generous amount of food that was given to us with Christmas dinner and the middle child's birthday all thrown in.

The second visit to Aldi was supposed to be a good one, one where I was going to have an hour of alone time to hang out in my favourite supermarket getting food to share with family and friends who I've not seen for a long time. I hadn't factored in that my heart had other plans, I now know what 'heart stings were pulled' means. Driving there was when I was reminded; how life was so different a few weeks ago; how my life has changed and the reason I was driving there. I listened to my heart and took a moment, but I knew that this was not a block stopping me from continuing with my plan, that I could think about that day while I got the food for the funeral, and I didn't have time to waste I needed to be back with the kids.

On week seven I was wandering around Tesco looking for treats to take to a friend's house, at this point I was eating sugar and treating myself with whatever I wanted, compared to Christmas time when I was so strict with the sugar I ate. Now, I felt the need to buy a chocolate cake with chocolate sauce, the type you put in the microwave, and it comes out all gooey and warm, it was one Joel's favourites. I wanted it but knew that an eight-portion cake was a bit too much and I was definitely not going to eat it all. I opted for a single portion golden syrup sponge with Cornish vanilla ice cream. I was going to devour it thinking of Joel, hoping that his spirit was hanging around for the event. I ended up having it for lunch one weekday, he would have loved the generous scoop of ice cream I ate for him. I wanted the food to trigger a positive thought in my heart. One where I could be connected to him for a while, remembering times we shared. I proceeded to order our favourite Indian and Thai over the next week and I visited his favourite French steak restaurant. It gave me so much joy amongst the remembrance.

It was September with the new school term beginning, I started to actively sort each messy corner of the house. Everything from kitchen cupboards to the loft ensuring the processes could be maintained and blocks sorted quickly. These processes, the clothes, uniform, food prep, lunch boxes, snacks etc were important as I didn't manage them well with my initial business that I started before my eldest was born in 2009. But the work life balance deteriorated as my workload increased and so did the number of children. The most work I had was when the boys were 2 years and 6 weeks old for five years until 2016. I then continued just managing my NHS service from home when the third child was born (2016). That NHS contract ended after 10 years in 2022.

Not having that work life balance resulted in a lot of stress for everyone. Joel looked after the boys when I was out of the house. A stay-at-home dad, one of the first back then in 2010. But I wasn't managing my work or my home life well. I didn't have the skills or support (as we now do through social media) to get through it in a positive way. I had to reduce the amount of front line work and focus on the home life. The kids were little and needed me. I learnt from that experience.

I decided that in order to get the perfect balance I needed to start my business with the job role of Cooking, Cleaning & Looking after the kids. I took it very seriously, working ten days straight at one point, and as a normal worker only taking two short breaks during the day. Joel would try to get me to take a longer lunch or go out, but I was adamant I was launching my businesses in January 2023 and needed to take action to complete this cleaning and clearing project.

After Joel died, I found the change of routine difficult, with the fridge and food preparation areas disrupted with so much extra food and treats. In order to cope I told myself not to worry about it. 'If food is wasted, if so much packaging is thrown away and the kids are eating takeaways a lot, it's ok, it's just for now, these things happen'. But maintaining the control of the sorting and cleaning was therapeutic, reminding me of what I had accomplished a few weeks before. I could do it again. And better this time. So, spoiler alert, six weeks in and the house is a mess and it's nice to leave it like that for a while, if no one's coming round, just leave it. Relax and I know I'm going to master it soon enough.

So, I'd been sorting the house out for two months getting ready for Santa to visit and I heard from Mariah Carey that 'the Lord is coming' so I was working hard! Did you know Santa knows stuff, he sees you when you're sleeping, he knows when awake, I really had to crack on. The fake Christmas tree was up on November the 1st and so was the

Christmas music! I was motivated and enjoying life. My business preparations were moving forward too, I had been to an overnight Audiology conference, to a Business show at the Excel centre and a new tech wax removal course. A lot had been achieved in those three months. I'd created and hosted two different websites myself, an E-commerce art site and informational wax removal site. My tax and admin were just about setup for me to do by myself. On a side note, yesterday I submitted my vat return on my own. I'm so proud!

I'm telling you all this to describe to you how ready I was for the future. The plans and actions I had already taken. Then Joel died. And I knew that my work could wait as there was actually no work. No one relying on me, no orders to fulfil, no invoices to be dealt with, I could just deal with life and what the universe has thrown us into and focus on the children and myself. I thought that we will remain calm and safe in the tornado that will encircle us. I think I managed it. Six weeks on and people keep asking me how the children are doing. I think they're doing well, they're able to interact as usual, eat well, sleep and play. Maybe time will show changes but I'm just trying to make time for all the things that help with releasing negative energy, getting more positive energy and being resilient, hardworking and calm.

CHAPTER 5:

The Messages & Support

A whole chapter on messages. A whole period where nearly everyone I've ever known contacted me with their condolences, their messages of love and support; I was uplifted and empowered by them. I felt the love from every single message and used it to move forward knowing that people all over the world were cheering me on, thinking positive thoughts about me and hoping that I would have the strength to keep my head up. I used all of that energy for myself and my children. I've never been part of anything like it. I have to admit the phrase 'media circus' came to mind but it wasn't a circus, it was respite; when bad things happen, your community does 'have your back'.

From the moment I knew I had to call my brother-in-law and tell him the bad news; I knew that I had started pushing a snowball and it was going to get big. Then calling my sister and parents, who then told my brother, and my brother-in-law told his family. From there the message was shared on WhatsApp groups and the news was out.

That first and second day I decided to wait and not reply. To take a moment to take it all in myself. Be off the phone and with the kids. But the snowball was growing with the school communities knowing, friends and family on social media even LinkedIn knew. I was becoming overwhelmed but knew I wanted to reply to each and every one as if theirs was the only message I got. They had taken time to think of us, to think about their words (and emojis) and let me know I have their support. Of course, I wanted to show them how much it meant. I remember thinking (two weeks in) about the number of people who had messaged me, I started counting from the 8th of December, 251 over all platforms. I couldn't believe it, but more and more people messaging each day; the snowball was getting bigger. After the funeral I put a post-up on Instagram and Facebook, oh-my-gosh, by the end my count was up to 500. I was glad I got my new phone before I posted, it was much easier managing them all on a quicker device. I did end up spraining my thumb from messaging so much. My phone usage app told me I had spent about 24 hours in first three weeks on WhatsApp.

It was therapy for me, therapeutic to send multiple heart emojis and telling my story of how I'm managing. Letting people know that we were ok, that they didn't need to worry, that we are strong and using the love and support that everyone is giving to move forward. There were many types of messages, long, short, involved religion or spirituality, stories of their own losses, how they coped. I was amazed at how they detailed the types of support they offered especially from our school community, I felt so proud that these people were in my life at this sad time.

It became my job. I made sure I cleared all my message notifications, replying and conversing with a few people at a time. So many people didn't just send one message, they checked up every few days. It was lovely. I decided to make it my job, my 'grief' admin tasks. A way to practice my admin skills by replying and by keeping on top of it, I wasn't going to get overwhelmed. It was part of the bigger picture, I had to see it as a positive exercise. To repeatedly say phrases that made me feel good, for example, "thank you for your lovely message" as I felt so much gratitude. I also said that "I was moving forward positively" hoping they would also feel positive just reading it. But also reinforcing in my mind that I am moving forward positively. I used multiple heart and sparkle emojis, that's the love and light I received and then sent back. It was therapy interacting with people who were my closest family to old colleagues and childhood friends, people scattered all around the world. It was the most amazing experience to be reunited with people who I've not chatted to for years. It felt so special that they messaged me.

There were some people who had been through similar experiences and found the messages" unhelpful" or "too much", I felt sad for them, for me, I was uplifted and energised. I counted myself lucky that this happened in a time of established social media and instant messages. I was able to receive an immense amount of support very quickly. I imagined a time when the only way was visiting that person, I knew I didn't want many visitors so I was even more grateful that I could be connected to so many. Guys, the cumulative effect of your messages of love and support were so powerful; I want to thank you again.

Currently I'm seven weeks in and am still receiving new messages and people are also checking up on me. It's all so very kind. I'm less job-like when replying, more like my usual self of leaving it for a few days as I compile them in my head then forget to actually send them. I had a system though, "don't open it unless you have the time to reply". I also said to myself, "It's ok if you don't reply at all, no one is expecting you to reply", but I wanted to. It made me feel good.

With messages came memories; friends and family reminding me of their time spent with Joel. Memories are interesting, they're different for everyone, and they trigger other memories. Through the messages I was able to think deeply about Joel, our memories and moments with we shared, another form of therapy, rather than blocking them, embracing them. This alongside my hours spent looking through photos was very meaningful. I made myself remember both the good and difficult times. The good ones would uplift me, and hard times would remind me of how I got up again; this was empowering. See, therapy! I knew to heal you must look within yourself; I knew it would be hard, but I knew it would be worth it. I didn't block any emotions, but I did allocate time for them. Five minutes here and there, a song, a photo or any trigger. I made time to be with my thoughts, memories and emotions; I felt connected to him, closer, believing that his spirit was around and his energy with us. Triggers could not be planned but when they happened, I was grateful for it, grateful to be thrown into a moment where emotion takes over, even for a split second; it's hard.

PART II:
HOW I GOT BACK UP AGAIN

CHAPTER 6:

Finding Contentment Post Pandemic

Our life wasn't all rosy, we didn't have the perfect life, life was difficult in lots of ways. I'm not going to go into it. But I want to convey that my mindset, physical and mental health were not at their best.

I decided that I needed to change things. Having always believed in the power of the Universe I delved into that first. I learnt that we can change what happens to us by the power of thought, of course action in the right direction is required too. We are all made up of energy, every cell in our body is vibrating. These vibrations can move the air around us and they keep radiating out into the universe. By having a high positive vibration, we attract it too. So, if we have positive energy, positive energy is attracted to us.

That was all well and good but how was I going to get positive energy? I thought exercise would be one but that was probably not going to happen unless you count walking a bit more. So, what else could I do? I kept going and found some information about how to be happy. I guessed that meant positive. It said I needed to do community work, to help the people around me and better their lives for no personal benefit apart from raising my vibration.

I had just been to the Coppetts Wood Festival in 2021 and found out about volunteering. The kids and I started going every Sunday at 9am for a few hours. It was fantastic, so therapeutic being out early in Autumn and working hard getting stuck into raking, digging, sawing, moving huge trees, making barriers and lots more, the boys especially loved the dangerous work! The text I read was right it was making me feel good. Looking after and maintaining our local nature reserve when they relied on volunteers was empowering to be part of. As the winter came it was harder to convince the kids to go so we stopped. I went alone a few times, but Joel didn't really look after the kids on his own at that point. It didn't stop me though. I decided to take some action in the direction I wanted to go in. The next summer festival (2022) was being planned and I mentioned that branded products would be a great way to raise more money. I am partial to buying a souvenir or two; I knew plenty of other people would be too. I've not mentioned but I've an addiction to stationary, art and craft supplies and anything to do with making stuff. I said I was able to source, make and sell the items at the festival. Joel was kind enough to donate the supplies so that relieved the pressure from making any sales! So, I set to work, in the end I made water bottles, notebooks, hand finished greeting cards, framed artwork, t-shirts and bags. It was the highest revenue stall; I was so pleased that I managed to raise that money for them. Joel was to help make the BBQ food but unfortunately my mother-in-law had died two days before and with his leg in a moon boot too, it was too much, but he would have been great at it and would have loved to join in too.

Another community volunteering opportunity arose during the Queens Golden Jubilee period. Our estate, made up of five roads were planning another street party. Joel suggested I should go and find out more information. I didn't want to at first as I knew that I may not have time to commit especially as I may get carried away with what I could offer. I went along with him and somehow signed myself up to design the leaflets, print and help distribute them. But also oversee the cake competition and make the prizes. I'll just say I killed two birds with one stone with this, I said that if the money raised goes to Coppetts Wood Conservationists then I'll do it. They said half the money, I was happy, so win-win in my book. I could feel my vibrations rising!

There were two leaflets, one where the kids and I with some of the team delivered to our roads, but the second one I delivered by myself. Ten thousand steps done, and I called that my exercise for the day! The party was a success! I somehow won the adults cake competition, I'll let you know a secret, I used the Tesco cake box, and somehow it was more delicious than people who, I'm sure, spent a long time making theirs. I had given myself the role of official photographer for the day and made a five-minute video of the event with lots of pictures of all the neighbours and the fun we had. After lockdown it was even more joyous to be surrounded by my community so I wanted to document that beautiful memory and share it. The team had said that it wouldn't have happened without my contribution and energy, I was so proud. I guess that's what happens with positive energy, it does come back to us.

The way I've continued my community work is through the woods. I was elected as a core member of the team where my role is social media, email and website management and also festival planning. As you can see these things don't involve going to the woods but rather my phone. I can still contribute and be with my kids without doing the heavy Sunday morning work. Recently we've started a one-hour Friday morning patrol through the woods, litter picking and planning. So I am getting the fresh air and steps in while the kids are at school. I've managed to squeeze the time in without affecting my family life. Doing good helps to raise your vibration but I knew it must fit into my life otherwise the stress starts to reduce the positive energy.

The next thing I learnt about happiness and being content was learning to do something, improving on an ability, practicing something daily. The previous year I tried a piano app, I used it for the first six months of the year. But not one to give up on a dream I decided to try a different one. This time I was going to learn how to play the piano, learn to sing and play the ukulele all from one app. It gave me so much joy to get good at something, trying my best to be dedicated to a cause and then hopefully instilling a drive in the children too. Full disclosure: I've not opened the app since September (it's now January). But that's ok, every day I aim to give it another go.

I was completely devoted to creating art over the summer, I wanted to practice my skill of drawing mandalas, the same thing over and over again. Practicing increasing my speed whilst maintaining the precision with the children around me, working on the stairs near their rooms or at the kitchen table or on the floor. Dedicated to creating a body of work that I could be proud of. I took no photos of the completed pieces or videos of the process. It would take up my precious time and distract me from the aim of creating the work. By the end of the summer, I had made over thirty pieces from A5 to A2. I had them scanned and uploaded them on to my website ready to sell. I was so proud of myself. Isn't that an aim in life, to be proud of yourself, not needing any verification from others just you and only your opinion matters?

During 2022 I worked hard to increase my confidence in my abilities to work consistently, to push myself when I wasn't motivated and achieve and congratulate myself on every single goal I reached. Before you get the wrong idea, I'd congratulate myself on filling the dishwasher, if I did it twice that day I'd be over the moon. If I made meals from scratch and didn't resort to the easy choice of takeaway, then a big pat on my back. Every little thing I said, "well done", I didn't need anyone else to say it. During the previous three months, from September, I stopped drinking tea and coffee as I felt I was being dictated by my addiction to them and I reduced my sugar intake significantly, these two things significantly affected my ability to sleep and the choices I made with food became positive. I also decided that I was addicted to Netflix so I somehow stopped that and replaced it with educational or business programmes and podcasts (Spotify told me that in 2022 I listened to 5000 hours of Steven Bartlett's podcast!). I was set up to cope and manage with what was to come on the 8th of December. My brain was geared up to be self-congratulating, fierce with my ideas about what I should eat and drink and how I wanted my future to pan out. I ran with it, I used my voice and was strong, I didn't allow anyone to get in my way. I knew myself and my children the best. 'Everyone better step out of the way, mum's in charge now!'

At seven weeks into being a widow and a single parent to three children I see things differently from the first month. I realise I was in fight mode not flight but stay and fight and show that I'm able to manage my children, able to manage my home, able to manage my messages and organise an event at home. I needed to prove that I could, to myself and to the people around me. Now at seven weeks in I've gone for flight mode, not given up but let go of the restrictions I put on myself. The house is a mess, I've not kept up to date with school things for the children, I've spent a small fortune on takeaways in the past two weeks, I now watch TV, drink tea and eat cakes. And I'm ok with it, no one is seeing my mess and the children are fed and watered and are thriving at school (all of them have got Star of the week in January). I'm taking time for myself eating Haagen Daz from the tub and writing my book, grieving through it and healing from it. I've got two days before I need to submit it and then I'll close this chapter and start the next one. It's not fight or flight mode but tried and tested; daily commitment to goals (home, children, work and self-love), exercise (closing my rings) and socialising (I'm now a lady who lunches with my lovely support network). I'm ready for the next chapter, I'm ready to accept my situation and I am going to keep moving forward.

CHAPTER 7:

Songs That Saved Me

There was one moment that was poignant in my journey, something that pivoted on my decision to stop and play this song. That moment was a week or so in, family were around and helping in the kitchen. They of course didn't know that my bin had a design fault where it's hard to get the black bag out if items have been squeezed in and the bag is heavy. Well, this happened, and I was trying late in the evening to change the bin and the bag was tearing and bits of the stuff I'd just swept were on top threatening to fall out everywhere! I could feel my calm disappearing and started seeing red. I stopped, took a breath, picked up my phone and played this song. Just with the intro music and during the first line, the bag slipped out like butter! I couldn't believe it. That's when I really believed in the magic of a positive mindset.

I want to talk and sing you through the song and others that help lift me, comfort me and empower me. The lines in italics are the ones I say to myself when listening to the songs. Which songs empower you? Add them to the Get Back Up Again playlist on Spotify.

'Get Back Up Again'

Get Back Up Again By Anna Kendrick

(Trolls Original Motion Picture Soundtrack)
Villa 40/RCA Records

'I really hope I can do it'

Starting with a positive mindset helps with any task (see back for more advice)

'Cause they're all depending on me'

I've got three kids and three cats and they're definitely depending on me but I'm also depending on me.

'I know that I must leave the only home I've ever known'

Getting out of my comfort zone will be tough

'And brave the dangers of the forest'

And do things I've never done before or say things that need to be said

'Saving them before they're eaten'

Before I lose what I've already built up

'I mean, how hard can that be?'

If I take one step at a time, how hard can it be?

'Looking up at a sunny sky, so shiny and blue and there's a butterfly'

I've got so much to be appreciative for I need to look up and see it.

'Well, isn't that a super fantastic sign'

I've definitely seen the signs, I'm ready now,

'It's gonna be a fantastic day'

It's going to be a fantastic day!

'Such marvelousness'

I'm going to find lots to be grateful for

'It's gonna bring, got a pocket full of songs that I'm gonna sing'

Yes, I'm going to keep singing and that will work

'And I'm ready to take on anything'

I can do anything I want; I am able to do it.

'Hooray!'

'Some super fun surprise around each corner'

Yes, don't we know, life is full of surprises,

'Just riding on a rainbow, I'm gonna be okay'

I'm going to see the beautiful light around me
and I'm going to be ok.

'Hey! I'm not giving up today'

I am definitely not giving up today!

'There's nothing getting in my way'

I'm able to do it,

'And if you knock knock me over'

Yes, you try and knock me down,

'I will *get back up again*, oh'

And you watch me get back up again!

'If something goes a little wrong'

I'm used to things going wrong so,

'Well you can go ahead and bring it on'

Bring it on, I've got the skills to overcome problems,

''Cause if you knock knock me over, I will *get back up again*'

I will *get back up again*!

'Whoa oh oh oh oh, *get back up again*,
whoa oh oh oh oh oh'

'I'm marching along I got confidence'

Ok, maybe it's imposter syndrome but I've got this, I can do it.

'I'm cooler than a pack of peppermints'

Yeah, I'd say!

'And I haven't been this excited since'

Yeah, it's been hard

'I can't remember when!'

*Yes, I do, as I'm doing well and
find excitement in lots of things.*

'I'm off on this remarkable adventure'

I love adventures,

'Just riding on a rainbow'

Just imagine, wouldn't it be amazing!

'What if it's all a big mistake'

Ok, self-doubt always comes in

'What if it's more than I can take'

Will I be able to do it?
'No I can't think that way 'cause I know that'
Yes, you're right, I can't think that way,
'I'm really, really, really gonna be okay'
Yes, I'm really, really going to be okay!

Million Dreams

In 2017 I took the children to a special showing with red carpet entertainment, food and goodie bags for The Greatest showman movie. A friend shared that anyone could actually turn up and you didn't need to be a member. I mean, I had a one-, six- and eight-year-old, but I wanted to go, I wanted that goodie bag! It was fantastic, with themed canapés, circus performers and free popcorn and cocktails during the movie; this was at the Everyman, Muswell Hill. I really enjoyed myself even though it was hard work and a lot of effort, but I remember that evening to be a good one.

This song sings to me. I do feel crazy with my wild ideas and belief in myself and wonder how I'm going to do it. But then if as the lyrics say, it's only going to take a 'million dreams', then I'm in for the ride, let's go and dive into those "brightest colours".

"In a world where we design" this lyric became so important after firstly watching A Handmaids Tale (watched 4 seasons back-to-back) and a few months later the death of Mahsa Amini. My mind was blown, I was already influenced by the sadness that Covid brought and felt that life was precious but understanding that I as a woman I can have my rights taken away in 2022 it was deeply saddening. I live in a place where I can take control of my life in any way I choose. No one is restricting me apart from myself. As I said, I binge watched A Handmaids tale and basically became so strong and independent (like June) as I wanted to make sure I truly appreciated the effort women have made in the past. I want to be one of those women who brake barriers. And if it only takes a million dreams then I'm going to sleep now! Let's dream big guys. "Now close your eyes" and see.

Million Dreams
by Pink (Atlantic Records)

'I close my eyes and I can see'

I will close my eyes, take a breath and see

'The world that's waiting up for me'

Woah yes I see that world, I'm there, looking good girl!

'That I call my own'

That's exactly what I want

'Through the dark, through the door'

I know it's going to be hard; I will have to create lots of opportunities to open doors and some might be the wrong ones

'Through where no one's been before'

I've got to try and see where I end up

'But it feels like home'

I really want to do it

'They can say, they can say it all sounds crazy'

Yep, people have literally said I'm crazy

'They can say, they can say I've lost my mind'

Go ahead,

'I don't care, I don't care, so call me crazy'

I don't care. I'm not crazy

'We can live in a world that we design'

I'm going to design my life

''Cause every night I lie in bed'

I think about this all the time

'The brightest colours fill my head'
I've got so many ideas, dreams and plans
'A million dreams are keeping me awake'
A million things I want to do
'I think of what the world could be'
I see who I could become, I see what I could create
'A vision of the one I see'
I've got a plan
'A million dreams is all it's gonna take'
Ok, let's go, a million thoughts
'Oh, a million dreams for the world we're gonna make'
A million dreams and a load of action and I'm going to make it!

Step by step

This was not one of my go-to songs, I discovered it when I asked family and friends to contribute to the Spotify playlist. It's uplifting, encouraging a positive mindset but acknowledging how difficult the journey is. It lays out exactly how to achieve your plans (getting over the bridge and through the river).

Step by Step
By Whitney Houston (Arista)

'Well there's a bridge and there's a river that
I still must cross'

After my husband died this is exactly what I felt, but I was in a boat not wading through the river. I'd already had the boat. I was so grateful to have my positive mindset, family support and all of what Joel had created for us.

'As I'm going on my journey'

I'm on my journey with my three children
and that's all that matters

'Oh, I might be lost'

I'm so glad I had already started an action plan and was mid-way through, I might be lost but I've got a map

'And there's a road I have to follow, a place I have to go'

There're some things I need to do, I need to grieve and accept and then I'll follow my map

'Well no-one told me just how to get there'

I'm making it up as I go along

'But when I get there, I'll know'

But I know how to do it, I know what I see as success

'Cause I'm taking it'

I've got a plan and

'Step by step, bit by bit'

Step by step

'Stone by stone (yeah), brick by brick (oh, yeah)'

One per cent by one per cent per day is enough

'Step by step, day by day, mile by mile (ooh, ooh, ooh)'

Take each day and keep trying,
keep going you're in for the long haul

'And this old road is rough and ruined'

I know it's going to be difficult facing the grief
and managing the children and house

'So many dangers along the way'

I've got lots of decisions to make on things I didn't know before

'So many burdens might fall upon me'

I've got more responsibility now

'So many troubles that I have to face'

They'll always be issues I need to deal with

'Oh, but I won't let my spirit fail me'

I won't let me spirit fail me

'Oh, I won't let my spirit go'

My spirit is strong

'Until I get to my destination'

I'm on the way

'I'm gonna take it slowly 'cause I'm making it mine'

One thing at a time

'Step by step, bit by bit'

I can do one step

'Stone by stone (yeah), brick by brick (oh, yeah)'

I can do one thing

'Step by step, day by day, mile by mile (ooh, ooh, ooh)'

I can keep going

'Say it, baby, don't give up'

Don't give up

'You got to hold on to what you got'

I'm grateful for what I have

'Oh, baby, don't give up'

I'm not giving up

'You got to keep on moving on don't stop (yeah yeah)'

Let's dance, move and keep going

'I know you're hurting, and I know you're blue'

It's really hard, life has changed there are so many triggers

'I know you're hurting but don't let the bad things get to' you'

But I am strong and I won't let the bad things get to me.

CHAPTER 8:

Positive Mindset: The Steps I Took

You can do it. A positive mindset will allow you to create goals, take action and get back up again if it all goes wrong. Simply changing the words, you use in daily life into positive words, forward thinking words, such as I will, I can, I will try. It will take resilience, ambition, hard work and creativity but step by step, just one per cent each day and you'll get there.

What does it actually mean? It means, are you a half full or half empty type of person? How you think about a situation makes all the difference in making it better. Being able to say, that's ok it's not the right time or I tried but I'll need to rethink or that was difficult I'm not ready yet. Acknowledging your effort and also using positive language to take the next step to improve will set your mind up to be calm and a rational thinker. I think it's important in every decision and thought I have. After a while it becomes very easy to spot a non-positive mindset.

My children are always taking about a growth mindset and their teachers drumming it into us that we need to learn about it for ourselves and our children. I immediately loved it. I'd already been a lover of the Power of Yet song on YouTube by Sesame Street and always thought I had a positive mindset. I was always able to see the bright side of a situation. But I actively started learning about it a year ago. This coincided with believing more in the universal energy, spirituality and understanding the scientific approach to happiness. A positive mindset was where I needed to start. I had always wanted to learn the piano and have done for the past 11 years but last year I decided to pay for an app and learn properly. I thought I could congratulate myself when I learnt and accepted when I didn't practice without putting any pressure on myself. Singing and music in general is known to play a positive influence in mental health and serotonin production.

I recently learnt the phrase 'toxic positivity', that's when you're not actually happy even though you're smiling. I could tell that some people thought I was doing that during the first month, I wasn't, I had plenty of time to be sad and not smiling. If there was an opportunity to smile, I would take it. There were some people I hadn't seen or spoken to for a long time, and it was so nice to see them. I enjoyed smiling and being happy that although in sad circumstances the joy was still there. The messages also made me smile. I smiled at each one, after all I needed that serotonin release.

Although I haven't been using the singing app, I have been singing. On the first night, I said to my brother-in-law that I must sing as soon as possible, I felt that the emotions of songs can be so powerful that I may not be able to do it. I knew I had to because it makes me feel so good to 'belt' out a ballad. I did sing the next day. I listened to the songs and I made sure I sang them. I later learned that singing activates the vagus nerve below the diaphragm which releases serotonin. I'm so glad I didn't become scared of singing. Singing along with writing unblocks the throat chakra which for me is a great form of therapy.

After having a positive mindset for a while, I turned to self-care and self-love. I took time out of looking after everyone else and had acupuncture and massage treatments, which in turn helped with my diet. In the past three months I had stopped tea and coffee, significantly reduced my sugar intake and tried to get my steps in. I felt like my mind was in a good place. I was taking care of myself, managing the house and family without stress and moving forward with my businesses. I was in such a good place with my mental health. It happened, Joel died but my spirit, one that he helped make, wasn't going to forget all that had been learnt. I was able to keep to a modified routine, executed Christmas as I had planned for the previous month. I just had to put everything I had ever learnt about managing situations like this into action. Even if that meant no action and sleep or rest and relax. My glass at that point was half full. I couldn't let it get any lower. I made sure that I was content with how each day went.

Positive Affirmations

I AM
ENOUGH

I AM A
GOOD
PERSON

TODAY, I AM
GRATEFUL

I CAN BE
ANYONE I
WANT TO BE

I MAKE MY
OWN CHOICES

I BELIEVE IN
MYSELF AND
MY ABLITIES

I AM
CREATIVE

BAD
EMOTIONS
WILL PASS

I AM GOING TO
GET THROUGH
THIS

I AM
CAPABLE

I WILL
BE OK

IT'S OKAY TO
BE SCARED

Positive Affirmations

I'M GOING TO MAKE TODAY COUNT

I AM EXTRAORDINARY

TODAY IS A FRESH START

THERE IS ALWAYS A REASON TO SMILE

I CAN MAKE A DIFFERENCE

I CAN AND I WILL

I HAVE PEOPLE WHO LOVE ME

I AM CAPABLE

BEING TRUE TO MYSELF IS WHAT MATTERS

TODAY I AM GRATEFUL

I DECIDE MY OWN ATTITUDE

MISTAKES ARE HOW GROW I GET BETTER EVERY SINGLE DAY

IT'S OKAY TO NOT KNOW EVERYTHING

CHAPTER 9:

Mindfulness And Positive Affirmations

Definition: Mindfulness [mind-ful-ness] noun 1. the quality or state of being conscious or awareness of something. 2. a mental state achieved by focusing one's awareness on the present moment, while calmly acknowledging and accepting one's feeling, thoughts and bodily sensations, used as a therapeutic technique.

I leant about mindfulness way back in 2008 when I was on my journey of managing a chronic pain condition called Fibromyalgia. I was to focus only on the pain, identify its location, the exact place inside my body, analyse the severity and type of pain. The focusing on it, accepting it and mentally massaging it away. Being there in that moment, focusing only on that task then moving on was initially a difficult thing to master. I've been learning since then attempting to put mindfulness into practice everyday, all day, in every part of my life. I understood this to be, 'thinking about or doing one task at a time'. I'm one who can multi-task so have millions of thoughts running through my mind. But slowing it down and doing one task well before thinking about the next was very helpful. I find that I can be free of 'all the things I need to do' Just one step at a time, one brick at a time, 'focus on the doing, not on the thinking about what I'm going to be do'.

I've heard meditation works well with mindfulness, practising being in a space thinking about one thing, chanting or focusing on breathing to help us become more aware of ourselves and our ability to sit and do one thing. I have always had the ambition to practice meditation, to wake up at 5am, I heard that's a good time for it, in the quiet before everyone wakes up. I've set my alarm for 5am so many times but every time snoozing it until 6am. I still think I'll manage it one day. Instead I try a few seconds or minutes here and there. Close my eyes and focus on my breathing. Calm down, rethink that if my mind is racing then I won't manage anything (I know not very 'growth mindset') but stopping for a second resets that thought back to 'one thing at a time'.

It works for me, that's how I've managed this situation. It's amazing how one can go from a 'messy' mind to a clear thinking one. All these decisions I've made over the last eight weeks have been made with a calm mind and little stress.

When there's no time to close my eyes and I'm in super busy mode with the kids I say these words to myself. Whichever pop into my head or ones relating to a task I need to do. For example, if I've got to load the dishwasher and I really don't like that task, I'll say 'I can do it, I am able, I will be grateful that I achieved it, it will benefit the whole house, I can do it'. Then I'll repeat as required or just sing the 'Get back up again' song by Trolls, the first two lines are "I really hope I can do it, 'cos they're all depending on me". If you're a parent then you'll know the daily thankless jobs we have to do. I need all the powers to get them done. Somehow it seems to work for me.

Currently, week eight, I'm in a place where all the dishes have been used and not washed, the clothes washing has piled up and there is stuff everywhere. I'm eating badly with takeaways and treats but I'm positive that this is part of the process of recovery and healing. I'm being kind to myself, just leaving the daily chores and writing my book (doing my therapy) and just 'keeping it simple'. The children don't seem to notice the plastic bowls being provided at breakfast or that they need to step over the things they've left on the floor. It's fine, I'm capable of doing it all, I'm just choosing not to. There will be a struggle to get back to a place where the house is tidy and processes are running smoothly. I'll probably have to print out the positive affirmation sheets (found on the next page) and put them on the frigde to read three times a day. Using my 'positive' playlist I will get motivated to make better choices. I know I've achieved it before; I know I can do it again.

Back in 2018 I drew my first mandala, I found it to be a fantastic way to switch off from everything around me. Just focus down on each and every line and bump I was drawing. Over time I've really honed in my skills of drawing accurately and quickly but I need ultimate concentration skills too. I breathe through the strokes, listen to the sound of the pen against the paper, the music that's created from a repeated strokes, it's meditative, sends me into a trance sometimes. It's quite fun drawing lines and bumps and then looking up and discovering you've drawn something quite intricate and beautiful.

I'm excited to be offering mandala drawing workshops for adults and children. Teaching and then seeing the beautiful work that's produced all because they listened to me and seeing that they really enjoyed the process. The workshops start with getting relaxed with a range of drawing supplies, music and their imagination. To be wild with the crayons, free with the coloured pencils and then draw delicate lines with the fine liners. All with varying dramatic or peaceful music. I want to teach them that they can engage with the medium and use it to control their emotions. They then learnt how to draw repeated lines and bumps and used the compass to draw circles (trickier than it looks). Everyone is then let loose on creating their own mandala designs in whichever medium they like. I try to encourage people that mistakes can be covered up, making new designs out of the mistake or just to keep going and see if it's still visible at the end. I'm always reminding myself of that when I make mistakes, drawing mandalas or just in life.

My Instagram and YouTube accounts will have videos on the process from the workshops so look out for them during 2023.

Why don't you give it a try, it's great whilst watching TV (not subtitled as you'll need to be looking down most of the time!), or listening to music. Try it on the back of a junk mail envelope or on a receipt at a cafe. It's a good way to spend time instead of scrolling away.

Share your creations with me, I'd love to see what you made and how you felt.

MANDALAS

CHAPTER 10:

How To Find Help With Getting Back Up

My advice would be to talk to anyone about whatever you're going through. On my second trip to Aldi, when I got the funeral food, I started talking to the cashier, she had actually lost her husband 15 years before and had two children to look after. We chatted and the overwhelm I felt initially going into the store was lifted. People you don't know can also make you feel better. A quick chat or an in-depth conversation to a helpline all benefit. I wasn't much of a 'sharer' I kept things to myself, but during this journey as there was always someone around (in real life or in my messages) I could discuss my thoughts, just air them out. I didn't need to take advice nor was I asking for it. Just 'talking it out'. So, if you're feeling alone, don't. Strike up a conversation, let it out and feel better.

If there aren't any people around you, try online. There are countless Facebook groups, counsellors and life coaches sharing a lot of free information, your Doctor may also be able to help with connecting you to Charities and advice centres in your area.

Get Back Up Again: Coping with Grief':

My social media support is found on Facebook and Instagram: Get Back Up Again Book: Coping with grief

I've created a safe place where we can discuss our journeys, give support and energy to each other and find out more information on how to develop and use a positive and growth mindset, learn more about mindfulness and practical steps on how to get back up again.

This public account has lots of free information and advice on mindfulness, positive and growth mindset, beautiful images and quotes. Learn how to draw mandalas and release some stress. Sharing practical advice on how to get back up again.

Epilogue/Conclusion

You can get back up again and you will get back up again!

Keep your goals in mind, take one small step each day, congratulate yourself each time and then just keep going. Use your favourite songs to uplift you. Move a little more each day, choose the healthier option to eat and smile when you can. Each step you take towards a positive mindset will set you up to be able to cope with anything the Universe throws at you. Believe you can do it, and you will.

Acknowledgments

Firstly, I'd like to thank my children; without them I wouldn't be me. They've supported and helped me through this difficult time. I'm so proud of how they've behaved at home and school. Their resilience and hard work has been so inspiring.

Thank you to my closest family and friends for supporting me through this time, your help has meant I was able to move forward with grace. You took the pressures away allowing me to be free and take back control of my life.

Thank you to everyone who messaged me; I'm ever grateful to your collaborative energy.

Thank you to Joel for giving me the tools to move forward, for supporting my new plans and always being my biggest cheerleader.

Thank you to the Universe for having my back and giving me showers of positivity in a period of deep sadness. I trust that good things are going to happen to me.

Lastly, thank you for buying and reading this book. I'd love to know which part resonated with you.

About The Author

Anchal Prasher

Anchal Prasher is an Audiologist and Artist, she lives in North London with her three children and three cats. She ran her own Audiology/ Hearing aid business between 2008 and 2022 and had started planing her new art related business before she suddenly lost her husband aged 43.

Writing her first book about her journey over the eight weeks following his death was a form of therapy, a way to delve into her thoughts and the actions she took. She did 'Get Back Up Again' and hopes that others who find themselves in a sad or difficult situation can take some ideas away and implement them into their own lives. She's resilient, positive-minded and is ready to take on the next chapter without her husband but with her three children.

Printed in Great Britain
by Amazon

19372126R00052